HUNTING FOR FAMILY HISTORY

A GENEALOGY GUIDE

LINDA REISS VOLIN

COVER PHOTOGRAPH:
The Greenstein Family
c. 1899

THIS BOOK IS DEDICATED TO MY PARENTS...

to my mother, Anne Reiss, who cherished family, her students, and the written word.

to my father, Mitchell Reiss, who valued family, technology and performing scientific investigations to improve life for the generations to follow.

ACKNOWLEDGMENTS

Words of appreciation are being extended to those who had a role in the preparation of this book.

Special thanks go to Sharan Volin for her wonderful help getting this book ready to be submitted for publishing.

Encouragement by Martin Volin and Stan Volin has been greatly appreciated.

Thank you to Miette Volin for art suggestions.

I thank all my students who have shared interests in genealogy and have become involved in their personal family searches.

I offer appreciation to my ancestors whose lives were so interesting that they inspired me to write books encouraging more people to learn about their family backgrounds.

CONTENTS

		Page
A Message to You		8

1. How can you learn about your family's history?...........11
2. What makes interviews fun?............................. 31
3. How is it possible to create a family tree?.................. 38
4. What can you learn about an ancestor's birth, marriage, or death? 40
5. What was early United States immigration like? 47
6. Did a relative from another country become an American citizen?.......................................55
7. How can a census help you find where the family lived? 63
8. Will your relatives from the past be listed in a city directory? 70
9. Was anyone in the family a military person? 78
10. How could you find a newspaper article about a family member from the past? 85
11. What family information can you locate in Social Security records? 90
12. Will the National Archives have your family's information? 96
13. Where is the Family History Center and what could it have about your ancestors?........................103
Some Genealogy Sites on the Internet 109
Glossary 110
Answer Key..119

A MESSAGE TO YOU

You may ask "What is genealogy? Is it a subject like social studies, science, math, English, or a foreign language? Why should we learn it?"

Genealogy is a subject that combines all the regular subjects into one exciting experience. It includes social studies: history, geography, and politics. By studying genealogy, you are learning the history of your family. It will make the past come alive for you.

This book helps you to understand how your family traditions started and how they compare with what is practiced today. You can learn how families of long ago moved from place to place and the reasons they moved. Studying genealogy helps you gather information about the geography of the world…past and present. It helps you learn names of the areas where your ancestors lived and the laws they had to follow.

In this book, you will use skills learned in English classes and find the meanings of words used in genealogy research. The words in bold, *italic* print in the reading selections have their definitions in the glossary in the back of the book. There are steps for doing research in special places that have old newspapers, magazines, record books and unusual materials. You will be guided to search on the Internet and use computer programs to write about what you find.

There will be skills helping you realize how to ask family members and older friends about earlier days that give you guidance for writing their stories.

In addition, you will be prepared to use new language skills as you learn how to search for family facts recorded in English and/or other languages. Math practice helps you to figure out the years your relatives lived in different places and how long they were there. You will use art to create ways to show the lives of your family members, even though you never knew them. Included in this book are many types of puzzles and other activities related to each topic discussed. These are only a few of the ways that genealogy combines with your other school subjects.

This book will teach you how to be detectives and find all kinds of information about relatives whose names you may not even know today. You will soon feel like you really knew your great-great grandparents and your ancestors who lived before them. Have fun with "Hunting for Family History!"

1. How can you learn about your family history?

A. Write a sentence telling one way you think you can learn about your ancestors.

B. Read these vocabulary words or groups of words that could be used in discussions about the reading selection:

access
brick walls
deferred
devise
documents
elusive
evidence
genealogy
generation

C. Now read the paragraphs.

Are you confused about a ***strategy*** to use when you are looking for your family history? In this book you will find a lot of ways to do ***genealogy research***. You will feel like a detective and have fun.

A good way to start this project is to answer the questions on the "Family Talk" question sheet that you will find in this section of the book. Some answers will have to be ***deferred***, so leave blanks. You can fill in the blanks when you ***devise*** a ***system*** for doing your research.

Use different **resources**. Birth, marriage, and death *documents* give much information. If they are available at home or at a relative's home, you will be lucky. Add the information you find to your "Family Talk" sheets.

Look through your parents' or grandparents' address books. You will find names of husbands, wives, and their children. Learn how they are related to you. Add their information to your "Family Talk" pages.

Access and look through old family scrapbooks. Greeting cards and announcements for birthdays, anniversaries, graduations, and other events may have dates and comments. You can find interesting information in school yearbooks and autograph albums. Letters and old postcards may describe your relatives' trips. A family member might have had a diary or journal.

Plan personal interviews with older *generation* family members. Use recorders and cameras if the people you interview will agree. If you cannot speak to them in person, write letters or emails to ask questions. Send a blank copy of "Family Talk" for them to fill out and return to you. Make telephone calls to find their answers.

Look at old family photographs and slides. The people in the pictures may seem *elusive* but continue to search for information. Ask older relatives who might know something about the people, events, or locations in the pictures. They may help you get past dead ends or ***brick walls***. Maybe they can give you the ***evidence,*** proof that someone else correctly guessed the name of the mystery person. Ask if anyone has an old family movie.

Always be sure the information is ***reliable***. Keep a ***research log*** about the facts that you learn and where you learned the details. Fill in as many places as possible on your "Family Talk" sheets. These are a few of the many ways to learn about your family.

D. Choose any two unfamiliar vocabulary words or word groups from Section B. Write down the words and what you think each word or word group means.

E. List three vocabulary words or word groups that you do not know. Look in the glossary for the definitions. Write the meanings on the lines next to each word on your list.

F. Answer these questions.

1. The <u>main idea</u> of this reading selection is that
   a. birth, marriage and death documents give you much information.
   b. there are many research strategies to use when studying your family's history.
   c. you should always look at old family photographs and slides.
   d. a brick wall is there when you cannot go any further in your research.

2. A research log
   a. gives deferred information.
   b. accesses scrapbooks.
   c. tells facts that you learned and where you found the information.
   d. is elusive.

3. According to the passage
   a. there are a lot of ways to do genealogy research.
   b. address books are useless in the study of family history.
   c. brick walls are usually a red color.
   d. none of the above are true.

4. All of these activities help you to learn your family
    history <u>except</u>
        a. looking at birth, marriage, and death documents.
        b. searching through family scrapbooks.
        c. studying a building with brick walls.
        d. interviewing older family members

5. The author suggests that
        a. written information and pictures along with
        conversations can help you gather good information
        about your family.
        b. address books can provide you with the best
        information when you want to learn about your
        family's past.
        c. scrapbooks are especially amusing when you are
        anxious to find out about your family.
        d. sometimes cameras can help you pass
        brick walls in your search for family facts.

G. Do this genealogy word match.

Match each word or word group in Column A with the definition in Column B. Put the letter of the definition in Column B next to the number of the word(s) it matches in Column A. See the sample.

A	B
k 1. evidence	a. dead ends in genealogy research
2. devise	b. sources of information
3. elusive	c. average span of time between birth of parents and birth of their children
4. strategies	d. list of dates, sources, and findings
5. access	e. official papers
6. documents	f. to get into
7. research log	g. plans, methods
8. generation	h. hard to find
9. resources	i. to plan
10. brick walls	j. dependable
11. reliable	k. proof

H. Put any form of five of today's words or word groups into statements. Draw a line under the vocabulary word or words that you are using.

I. Place any form of five of today's words or word groups into questions you would ask a professional genealogist.

J. Write a paragraph that tells one interesting way to learn about your family history and why you chose to write about it.

K. Your friend wants to learn about a great-great-grandparent. She/He asked you if you would be able to help him/her find information. Write a friendly letter telling what she/he should do.

 L. Write a true <u>or</u> make-believe story for <u>one</u> of these titles:

"My Relative's Talking Address Book"

"The Postcard that Took Me into My Family's Past"

"Discovered in the Old Scrapbook"

"Secrets in the Attic"

"The Mystery of the Hidden Words"

M. See if you can do this crossword puzzle.

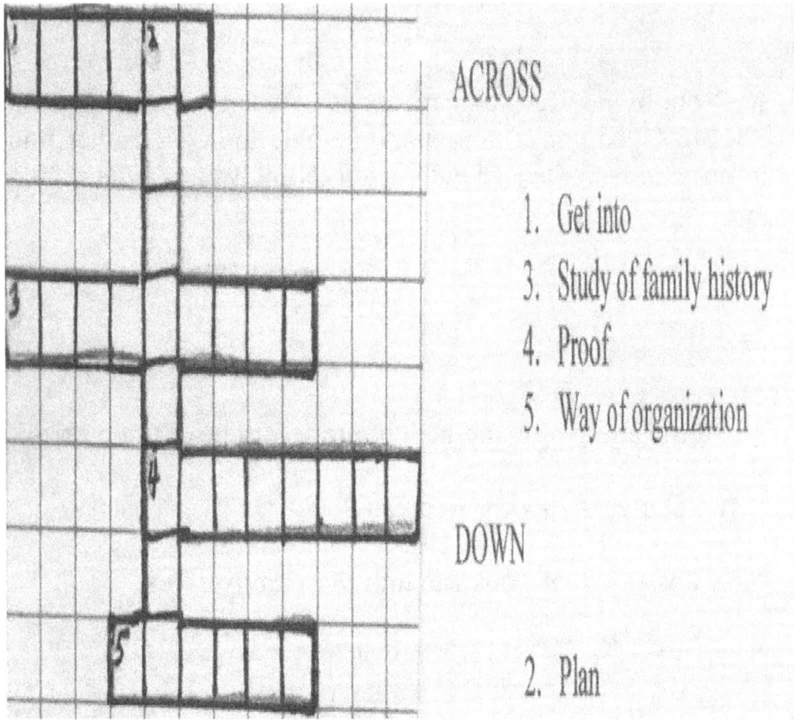

FAMILY TALK GENEALOGY QUESTIONNAIRE

What is today's date? _______________________

ABOUT YOU
What is your first name? _______________________

What is your middle name? _______________________

What is your last name? _______________________

When is your birthday? _______________________

Where were you born?   town ___________state _________
country _______________________

What language(s) do you speak most of the time?
____

What was the name of your first school?
____

Where was your first school?
____

What country was it in?
____

When did you go to that school?
____

What other school(s) have you attended?

____

What is/are the location(s)?
____

What do/did you like to do after school?
____

____

Do you have any sisters?
____

What are their names and ages?
____

____

How old are they?
____

Do you have any brothers? _________

What are their names and ages?
____

____

ABOUT YOUR MOTHER

What is your mother's last name? _________________________

What is her first name? _______________________

What is her middle name? ______________________

When was she born?

month________day_____________year_________

Where was she born? town________________state_______

country ____________________

What language(s) does she speak?

____

What were the names of her schools?

____

Where were her schools?

____

What were the names of towns, cities, and countries where she lived? ____

If she was not born in this country, how old was she when she came here? _____

Who came to this country with her?

____

What job(s) does, or did she have?

____

What did she like to do for fun when she was a child?

____

Who are her sisters and brothers?

____

ABOUT YOUR FATHER

What is your father's last name? ___________________________

What is his first name? ___________________________

What is his middle name? ___________________________

When was he born?   month __________ day ___ year ___

Where was he born?   town __________   state __________
country __________

What language(s) does he speak?

____

What were the names of his schools?

____

Where were his schools?

____

____

What were the names of towns, cities, and countries where he
lived? ___________________________

____

If he was not born in this country, how old was he when he
came here? __________
Who came to this country with him?

____

____

What job(s) does, or did he have?

____

____

What did he like to do for fun when he was a child?

____

____

Who are his sisters or brothers?

____

**ABOUT YOUR MOTHER'S MOTHER
(YOUR GRANDMOTHER)**

What is your mother's mom's last name? _____________

What is your mother's mom's first name? _____________

What was her last name when she was born? __________

When was she born? month _________day____ year___

Where was she born? town________ state_____country _____

What is her husband's name? _______________________

Where did they get married? _______________________

If she was not born in this country, how old was she when she came here?____________________

Where did she live when she first came here?

____

Who came here with her?

____

What was her first language?

____

What other languages does she speak?

____

What were the names of her schools?

____

____

Where were her schools?

____

What job(s) does/did she have?

____

What did she do for fun as a child?

____

What did she do for fun when she got older?

____

ABOUT YOUR MOTHER'S FATHER
(YOUR GRANDFATHER)

What is your mother's father's last name?

____

What is your mother's father's first name? ______________
When was he born? month_______ day_____________ year ___
Where was he born? town_______ state_______ country_____
If he was not born in this country, how old was he when he
came here? ___________
Where did he live when he first came here?

____

Who came here with him?

____

____

What was his first language?

_______________________________________ __ __

What other languages does he speak?

____

What were the names of his schools?

____

Where were his schools?

____

What job(s) does/did he have?

____

____

What did he do for fun as a child?

____

____

What did he do for fun when he got older?

____

ABOUT YOUR FATHER'S MOTHER
(YOUR GRANDMOTHER)

What is your father's mother's last name? _______________

What is your father's mother's first name? _______________

What was her last name when she was born?

____

When was she born? month __________ day__________ year

Where was she born? town ______state ______ country ______

What is her husband's name? _______________________

Where did they get married? _______________________

If she was not born in this country, how old was she when
she came here? ______

Where did she live when she first came here?

____

Who came here with her? _______________________

What was her first language?

____

What other languages does she speak?

____

What were the names of her schools?

____

Where were her schools?

____

What job(s) did, or does she have?

____

What did she do for fun as a child?

____

____

What did she do for fun when she got older?

____

ABOUT YOUR FATHER'S FATHER
(YOUR GRANDFATHER)

What is your father's dad's last name?

____

When was he born? month _____ day _________ year_____

Where was he born? town ___state _______ country ______

If he was not born in this country, how old was he when he came here? ________________

Where did he live when he first came here?

____

Who came here with him?

____

What was his first language?

____

What other languages does he speak?

____

What were the names of his schools?

____

Where were his schools?

____

What job(s) did, or does he have?

____

What did he do for fun as a child?

____

____

What did he do for fun when he got older?

____

____

ABOUT YOUR MOTHER'S GRANDMOTHER (YOUR GREAT-GRANDMOTHER)

What is your mother's grandmother's last name?

____

What is your mother's grandmother's first name?

____

What was her last name when she was born?

____

When was she born? month ____day __year ____
Where was she born? town ______state______ country _____
What was her husband's name? ___________________________
Where did they get married? ____________________________
If she was not born in this country, how old was she when she came here? ___
Where did she live when she first came here?

____

Who came here with her?

____

What was her first language? ___________________________
What other languages did she speak?____________________
What were the names of her schools?

____

Where were her schools?

____

What jobs did she have?

____

What did she do for fun as a child?

____

What did she do for fun when she got older?

____

ABOUT YOUR MOTHER'S GRANDFATHER
(YOUR GREAT- GRANDFATHER)

What is your mother's grandfather's last name?

____

What is your mother's grandfather's first name?

____

When was he born? month ___ day____ year ______
Where was he born? town______state______country ______
If he was not born in this country, how old was he when he came here? _______________
Where did he live when he first came here?

____

Who came here with him?

____

What was his first language?

____

What other languages did he speak?

____

What were the names of his schools?

____

Where were his schools?

____

What job(s) did he have?

____

____

What did he do for fun as a child?

____

What did he do for fun when he got older?

____

ABOUT YOUR FATHER'S GRANDMOTHER (YOUR GREAT-GRANDMOTHER)

What is your father's grandmother's last name?

____

What is your father's grandmother's first name?

____

What was her last name when she was born?

____

When was she born? month ___ day ___ year ________
Where was she born? town _______ state ___ country ______
What was her husband's name? ___________________
Where did they get married? _____________________
If she was not born in this country, how old was she when she came here? ____
Where did she live when she first came here?

____

Who came here with her?

____

What was her first language? ___________________
What other languages did she speak?______________
What were the names of her schools?

____

Where were her schools?

____

What job(s) did she have?

____

What did she do for fun as a child?

____

What did she do for fun when she got older?

____

ABOUT YOUR FATHER'S GRANDFATHER (YOUR GREAT-GRANDFATHER)

What is your father's grandfather's last name?

____

What is your father's grandfather's first name?

____

When was he born? month _______ day_______year_______
Where was he born? town ______ state ___country ________
If he was not born in this country, how old was he when he came here? _____
Where did he live when he first came here?

____

Who came here with him? _________________________

____

What was his first language?

____

What other languages did he speak?

____

What were the names of his schools?

____

Where were his schools?

____

What job(s) did he have?

____

What did he do for fun as a child?

____

What did he do for fun when he got older?

____

1. *What makes interviews fun?*

A. Think about a story your relative told you about his or her younger days. Write a sentence about it.

B. Read these words or groups of words that could be used in discussions about the reading selection:

alluding to
articulate
chronological order
documents
investigation
revelations
siblings
truisms

C. Now read the paragraphs.

In your *investigation* of your family history, how do you think you can ask a person to give you many details? Prepared interviewers can get lots of information. You should list questions before the meeting and give your relative an idea of what you will want to talk about during the meeting and why. Tell the person that you will show him or her anything that you write about the interview. Say it will have *truisms* that he or she told you. Ask if they will let you record the interview. If the person does not agree, plan to write down important facts. Have the question session for one hour.

Meet in a quiet place. Do not eat during the meeting. Try to memorize the first two questions on your list. That will make him or her feel comfortable. Start with a question or topic that you know will get the person to talk. It can **pertain to** something you heard your relative tell in the past.

Articulate clear, easy-to-understand questions that would have long answers. Good questions begin with "How" and "Why." Other questions that have long answers may begin with "What happened when…." and "What made you decide to..." Do <u>not</u> **pose questions** that require simple yes or no answers. Talk about his or her **siblings.** You may get interesting **revelations**. Ask for examples.

Listen carefully. As the person talks, ask questions **alluding to** what the person discussed. Let him or her talk freely.

Show old photographs, ***documents,*** and old items to help bring back memories. Let your relative talk about things that are not on your question list. After the interview you can put the comments in ***chronological order***. Look at the person's facial expressions and ***mannerisms*** as he or she is being interviewed.

Be polite. Do not interrupt the person. Keep him or her relaxed. Be open and honest about what you are doing. Have the relative feel happy to share in this joint project to collect and save his or her memories.

If the person is tired or losing interest, end the interview. Remember to thank the person for an interesting meeting. By following these suggestions, you will have an interview that has been fun and will be a fine record in your family history project.

D. Write any two vocabulary words or word groups that interest you in the reading selection. Next to each one write what you think the meaning is.

E. List three vocabulary words or word groups that you do not know. Look in the glossary for the definitions. Put the meanings next to each word on your list.

F. Find the answers to these questions:
1. The <u>main idea</u> of this reading selection is that you should
      a. plan to have interviews in quiet places.
      b. show documents and old photographs whenever you can.
      c. listen carefully so you will not forget the person's comments.
      d. be well-prepared when you are going to interview someone.

2. A sibling is someone's
    a. document.
    b. chronological order.
    c. revelation.
    d. brother or sister

3. According to the passage
    a. it is good to prepare interview questions that require short answers.
    b. you should quickly interrupt your relative when you have a question during an interview.
    c. it is important for you to get as much information about the person you are interviewing, even if it takes a very long time.
    d. none of the above are true.

4. All of these are good rules to remember during interviews, except this:
    a. Ask questions that need *yes* or *no* answers.
    b. Speak clearly.
    c. Listen carefully.
    d. Thank the person for the interview.

5. The passage suggests that
   a. a long interview will bring out the best answers.
   b. you should offer food to the person you are interviewing so he or she will feel comfortable.
   c. the success of your interview will depend upon your planning and the way you treat the person you are interviewing.
   d. you should encourage the person to supply answers to your specific questions and not stray from the question.

G. Complete this genealogy word match.

Match each word/word group in Column A with the definition in Column B. Put the letter of the definition in Column B next to the number of the word(s) it matches in Column A. See sample.

A	B
e 1. truism	a. examination by systematic inquiry
2. alluding to	b. talk clearly
3. investigation	c. specific actions
4. document	d. ask questions
5. pose questions	e. something true
6. chronological order	f. brother or sister
7. sibling	g. was about
8. pertained to	h. in the order in which things happened
9. mannerisms	i. official paper
10. articulate	j. making indirect reference to
11. revelations	k. things that are revealed

H. Put any form of five of today's words or word groups into statements. Draw a line under the vocabulary word or words that you are using.

I. Place any form of five of today's words or word groups into questions to ask a famous person.

J. Your friend wants to know how to interview his or her grandmother. Write a paragraph about what you would recommend.

K. Write a letter to a friend, telling what you think are the three most important things to remember when you interview people. Give reasons for making those choices.

L. Write a true <u>or</u> make-believe story for one of these titles.

"An Interview with a Famous Person"

"The Magic Question that Made My Interview Great."

"The Story about the Mysterious Photograph"

"Lost in the Memory"

"An Unexpected Interview"

M. Figure out this crossword puzzle.

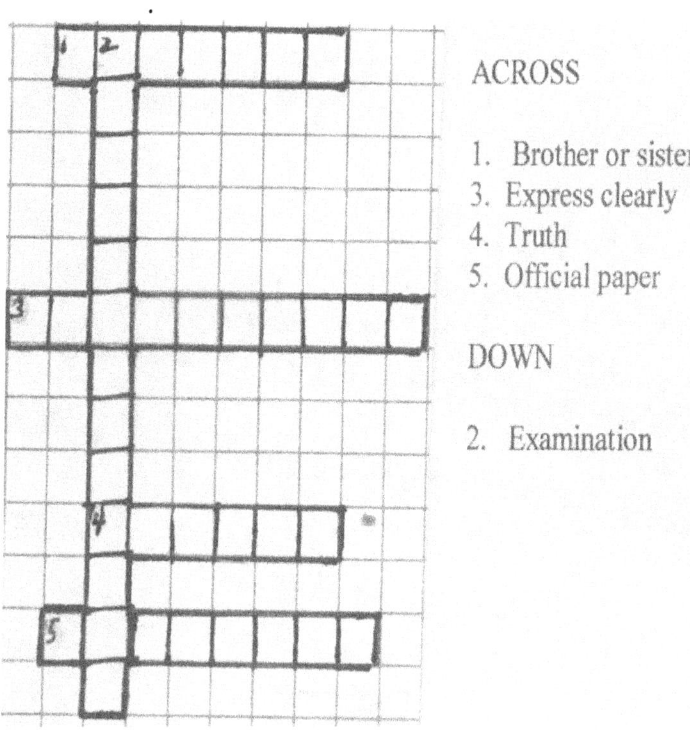

N. Collect information to place on the *FAMILY TALK* questionnaire.

O. Write about your plans to get more information.

3. *How is it possible to create a family tree?*

A. Look at the picture. What information do you see?

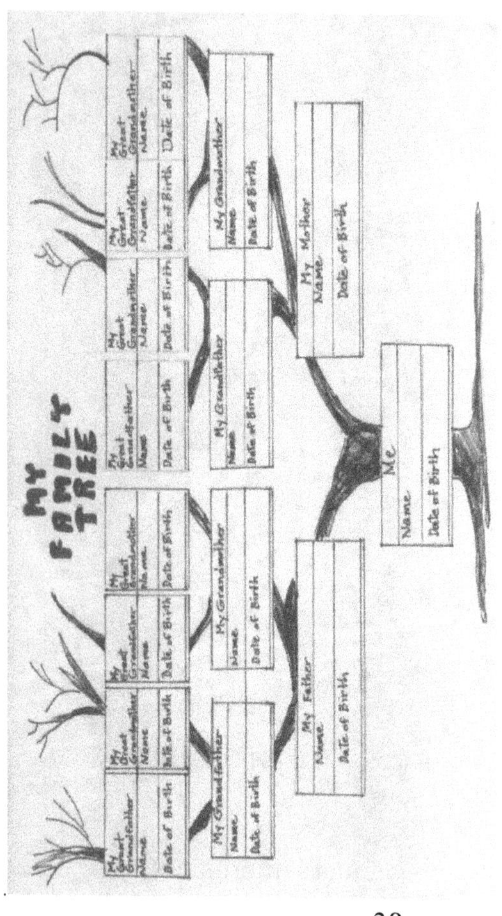

B. Now read the paragraphs.

The picture before these paragraphs is a type of *family tree*. It is a chart that shows the names and basic facts about all members of a family - from the oldest to the youngest.

When you gather family information, you could also record it in a **research log**. By keeping a research log up to date, you will have a record of what you know, plus where and how you found the information.

If you keep your genealogy information on a good chart of any type, you will see a clear picture of your family's history.

C. Have fun designing your own family tree. Leave the boxes empty. You'll fill them in when you gather information.

4. What can you learn about an ancestor's birth, marriage, or death?

A. What do you think has been the most important paper in your life? Place your idea, with reasons, in a sentence.

B. Read these words or groups of words that are used in discussions about the topic of this reading selection:

> affidavits
> anglicized
> composite picture
> conceal
> deliberate
> distort
> inadvertent
> informant
> mandate
> omission

C. Now read the paragraphs.

Official birth, death, marriage, and divorce records are known as **vital** records in the United States. They are the papers about the most important things that happen in a person's life. In some countries the important records are called Civil or Metrical records. They are **affidavits** by the **informant** that cannot have **deliberate omissions** of the facts. Information must not be **concealed** or **distorted.**

Today we cannot imagine being without these documents. However, many, many years ago there were no vital records. In 1789 France was the first European country to have civil registration of vital events. In the early 1800s Russia, Austria and Germany started to keep records. In the 1820s Russia's churches had birth certificates for babies of different religions. The United States was one of the latest countries to **mandate** that vital records be registered. Massachusetts started in the middle of the 1800s. Other states waited until the beginning of the 1900s. The country of Iran did not keep civil records of vital events until the end of the 1900s.

You can find vital records in libraries and archives. There are laws for getting copies of vital records from different places. When you look for vital records of immigrant relatives in the United States, remember that the name on the record may not be the **anglicized** name that you know. Look under different spellings. When you find your ancestors' vital records you will see that the special information will help you learn your family's history.

D. Pick any two vocabulary words or word groups from Section B. Write what you think the meaning is next to your word choices.

E. List three vocabulary words or word groups that are unfamiliar. Look in the glossary for the definitions. Write the meanings on the lines next to each word on your list.

F. Find the answers to these questions.

1. The <u>main idea</u> of this reading selection is that
      a. France was the first European country to have civil registration of important events.
      b. there are records to help you find information about family births, marriages, deaths, and divorces.
      c. you can find vital records in libraries and archives.
      d. Iran did not keep civil records of vital events until the end of the 1900s.

2. In some countries important records may be called
      a. affidavits.
      b. civil records.
      c. an anglicized name.
      d. telephone directory.

3. According to the passage
    a. divorce records are vital records.
    b. a birth certificate could be called a metrical record.
    c. some churches may have records from babies of
    different religions.
    d. all the above choices are correct.

4. All of the following facts are in the selection <u>except</u>
    a. Years ago there were no birth, marriage, or death
    records.
    b. The United States had vital records before most
    other countries.
    c. Iran did not have vital records until the end of the
    1900s.
    d. France was the first country in Europe to have vital
    records.

5. The reading selection suggests that
    a. you may not be able to find official birth records for
    some of your ancestors who lived in the 1600s.
    b. all names are spelled correctly on birth records.
    c. names on birth certificates are usually anglicized.
    d. all states in the United States started keeping vital
    records in the eighteenth century.

G. Complete this matching exercise.

Match each word or word group in Column A with the definition in Column B. Put the letter of the definition in Column B next to the number of the word(s) it matches in Column A. See the sample.

	A		B
b	1. evidence	a.	combination of details
	2. conceal	b.	proof
	3. composite picture	c.	person who gives facts
	4. mandate	d	something left out
	5. vital records	e.	order
	6. omission	f.	done on purpose
	7. deliberate	g.	birth, marriage, death records
	8. distort	h.	made to be like English
	9. informant	i.	to hide
	10. anglicized	j.	to twist

H. Put any form of five of today's words or word groups into statements. Put a line under the vocabulary word or words that you are using.

I. Place any form of five of today's words or word groups into questions you would ask someone who works in an office that has vital records.

J. Write a paragraph to tell what you think is most interesting in the passage about the history of vital records. Explain why you made that choice.

K. Write a letter to a friend, asking if he or she would like to meet you to search through vital records. Give reasons why it would be an interesting thing to do.

L. Write a true or make-believe story for one of these titles.

"The Vital Record that Spoke."

"Found, At Last!"

"Spelled a Different Way"

"A Search for Answers in the Vital Records"

"The Vital Record that was Hidden in the Old Book"

M. Enjoy this crossword puzzle.

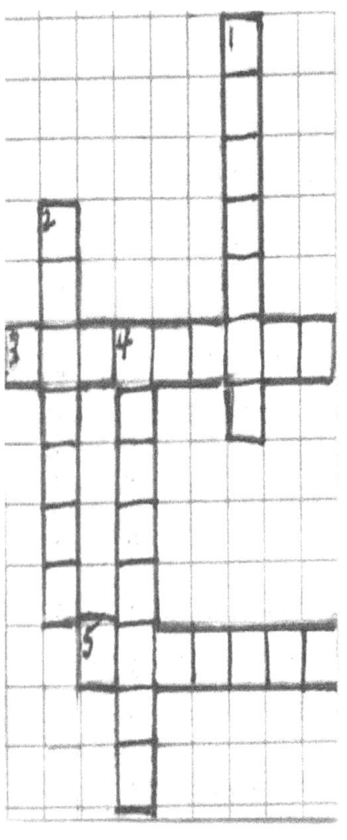

ACROSS

3. Person who gives information
5. Twist to mix up truth

DOWN

1. Hide
2. Order
3. Something left out

5. *What was early United States immigration like?*

A. Look at this picture.

Write a sentence that tells what you know about this statue.

B. Read these words or word groups that are in the reading
selection.

       alien
       detain
       embark
       final destination
       manifest
       marital status
       myth
       nationality
       naturalized
       occupation
       residence
       steamship

C. Now read the paragraphs.

    Your immigrant ancestors may have spotted this statue
if they sailed into New York Harbor toward Ellis Island. The
ship records kept on Ellis Island can certainly offer you much
information about your families who **embarked** on a
steamship to head for their **destination,** the United States of
America. Each traveler gave the shipping clerk information to
put on a form. There were details about his or her name,
marital status, **occupation, nationality,** and the person's

place of *residence.* Every person gave the name used in his or her region or country, not an American name.   Each *alien* worried about being *detained* before being allowed to set foot on the new soil… or being refused admission to the United States. Details of the person's entrance into the United States were further recorded when he or she was *naturalized.*

Many types of immigration records were kept through the years. In the 1800s they were called Customs Lists. At the end of the 19th century there were Passenger Arrival Lists, also called *manifests.* They gave more information than the Customs Lists.

Immigrants sailed into many ports in the United States. From 1855-1890 they entered Castle Garden in New York Harbor. On April 19, 1890, the Barge Office accepted the immigrants. Ellis Island opened on January 1, 1892. There was a fire on Ellis Island on June 14, 1897. Many records were ruined. Ellis Island received immigration again in December of 1900 and continued to serve as the major New York port until it closed on March 4, 1955. Immigrants sailed to other ports including Baltimore in Maryland; Boston in Massachusetts; Philadelphia, Pennsylvania; New Orleans, Louisiana and Galveston, Texas. Records for all these ports are on microfilm at the National Archives.

Some immigrants traveled across the Canada-United States border. If immigrants came directly to the United States, their names were on the United States manifests. If they went to Canada first, their information would be on microfilm at the National Archives of Canada.

When you search for ancestors, think of how the surname might have been spelled in the person's native country. Many people wanted to sound American, so they changed their names and their parents' names after living in the United States. It is a ***myth*** that names were changed at the ports of arrival.

When you try to find your ancestor in immigration records, you should guess the year of arrival and port of arrival. You could say he or she came ***circa*** 1891 or circa 1920. Good luck in your search for your family's immigration information!

D.   Write any two vocabulary words or word groups highlighted in the reading selection. Next to each one tell what you think the meaning is.

E. List three vocabulary words or word groups that you do not know. Look in the glossary for the definitions. Write the meanings next to each word on your list.

F. Find the answers to these questions.

1. The <u>main idea</u> of this reading selection is that
     a. ship records were at Ellis Island.
     b. there are different places to look for immigration information about your ancestors.
     c. Ellis Island closed in 1955.
     d. some immigrants came to the United States through the Canadian border.

2. A Passenger Arrival List is also called
     a. a naturalized document.
     b. an alien.
     c. a destination.
     d. a manifest.

3. According to the passage
     a. ship records were at Ellis Island.
     b. sometimes an alien was refused admission into the United States.
     c. some immigrants entered the United States through Canada.
     d. all the above choices are true.

4. Each of the following immigration facts are mentioned in the selection, <u>except</u>
  a. Customs Lists in the 1800s had many immigration records.
  b. People entered New York at Castle Garden from 1855-1890.
  c. Ellis Island closed its immigration office forever because of the big fire in 1897.
  d. Passenger Arrival Lists were also called manifests.

5. The author suggests that
  a. immigrants sailing across the ocean knew that America would accept them with open arms.
  b. not all our immigrant ancestors passed the Statue of Liberty as they entered the United States.
  c. The National Archives of Canada has only a small amount of information about your ancestors who came to America through Canada.
  d. Castle Garden was a colorful place to visit.

G. Complete this matching exercise.

Match each word or word group in Column A with the definition in Column B. Put the letter of the definition in Column B next to the number of the word(s) it matches in Column A.

       A   B

1. marital status   a. delay
2. occupation   b. became a citizen
3. nationality   c. a false belief
4. steamship   d. where one lives
5. residence   e. a ship that moves by steam
6. manifest   f. membership in a particular country
7. naturalized   g. tells whether a person is married or single

8. alien   h. passenger list
9. detain   i. type of work a person does
10. myth   j. someone who is a citizen of a different country

H. Place any form of five of today's words or word groups from Section B into statements. Put a line under the vocabulary word or words that you are using.

I. Write any form of five of today's new words or word groups into questions you would ask a person who does work with immigration records.

J. Prepare a paragraph to give a brief history of immigration as explained in the reading selection.

K. Create a short play, telling what you and another person are talking about as you enter the United States for the first time.

L. You are a new immigrant in 1900. Write the feelings you had when you saw the Statue of Liberty.

M. Complete the crossword puzzle.

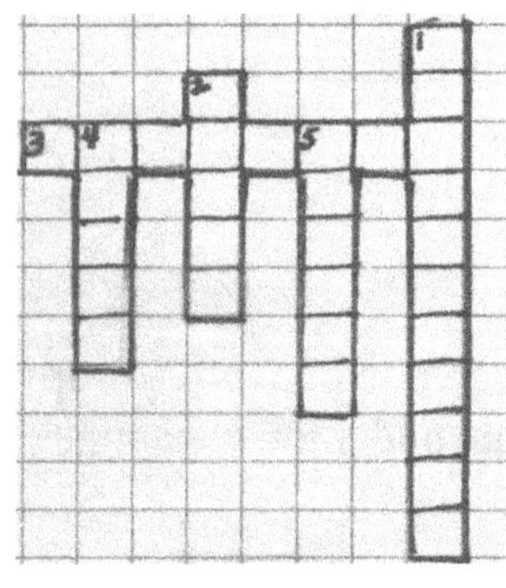

ACROSS

3. List of passengers

DOWN

1.   Membership in a particular nation
2.   Around
4. A foreign-born resident who is still a citizen of a foreign country
5. Go aboard a ship

6. *Did a relative from another country become an American citizen?*

A. Look at the Declaration of Intention, a paper completed for the process of becoming an American citizen.

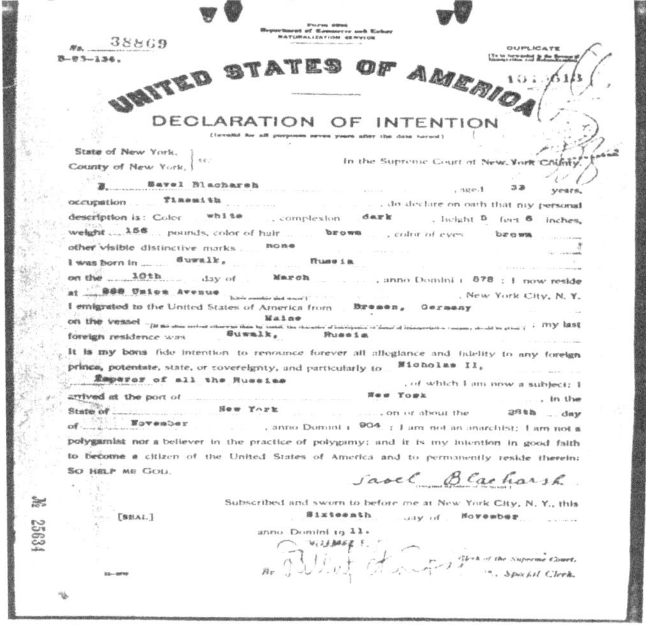

Write about the item that interests you the most and the reason for your choice.

B. Read these words or word groups that are used in the reading selection.

> Declaration of Intention
> declare
> freedom
> Freedom of Information Act
> intention
> naturalization
> notary
> petition
> verify

C. Now read the paragraphs.

Citizenship or ***naturalization*** records can give you a lot of information about your ancestors.   Your family members could have been naturalized in federal, state, or local courts. These records may have been kept at the court or transferred to a regional archives branch.

Types of naturalization records are the ***Declaration of Intention***, ***Petition*** for Naturalization and Certificate of Naturalization. Before looking for documents it is important to know where and the approximate year when the person could have become a citizen.   When your ancestor said he or she wanted to become a United States citizen the first papers were filled out. That was known as the ***Declaration of Intention.***   Information on this application were the person's name, country of birth, date of application and signature. Some may show the date and port of arrival in the United States. After 1906 there was a more detailed form showing the individual's age, occupation, and personal description. Also included were his or her present and last foreign address, port he or she sailed from, the name of the ship and date of arrival. A declaration was not needed if the applicant served and was honorably discharged from military service or had entered the United States as a child.

The Petition for Naturalization was used as a formal application for United States citizenship. Information on this form included: name, residence, occupation, date and place of birth and citizenship. Listed were the port and date of arrival, marital status, and other family information. There was also a personal description. After 1930 the petition had the applicant's picture. Witnesses had to *verify* that the comments of the applicant were true. The actual ***Certificate of Naturalization*** was given to the person.

You might be lucky enough to find your relatives' naturalization papers in your family's papers. If not, you can look in the various archives that will be discussed later in this book. You are entitled to have copies of the naturalization information under the ***Freedom of Information Act.***

D. Write any two vocabulary words or word groups from Part B. See if you can figure out the meanings from the way they are used in the reading selection. Next to each one tell what you think the meaning is.

E. List three vocabulary words or word groups that you do not know. Look in the glossary for the definitions. Write the meanings on the lines next to each word on your list.

F. Answer these questions.

1. The <u>main idea</u> of this reading selection is that
    a. the Declaration of Intention was an important paper signed by immigrants.
    b. the Certificate of Naturalization was given to the person who became a citizen of the United States.
    c. children did not sign a Declaration of Intention.
    d. you can locate an ancestor's naturalization records and find details about him or her.

2. The Declarations of Intention were
    a. the first papers that the immigrants completed when they wanted to become citizens.
    b. known as Freedom of Information Acts.
    c. honorable discharges from military service.
    d. the final papers for citizenship in the United States of America.

3. According to the passage
    a. people were naturalized in several types of courts.
    b. witnesses had to verify that the immigrant's information was true.
    c. you can have copies of a relative's naturalization documents.
    d. all the above are true.

4. The passage mentions all the following facts, <u>except</u>
    a. You can find naturalization records in more than
    one place.
    b. The first step towards U.S. citizenship was to file a
    Declaration of Intention.
    c. Naturalization records are different from
    citizenship records.
    d. The formal application for U.S. citizenship is
    known as the Petition for Naturalization.

5. The passage suggests that
    a. naturalization records can only be found in the court
    where the relative appeared.
    b. you could have a good chance of finding a copy of
    your ancestor's Certificate of Naturalization if you
    find his or her Petition for Naturalization.
    c. your relatives could only have been naturalized in
    Federal Courts.
    d. personal descriptions never appeared on the
    citizenship papers.

G. Have fun with this genealogy word search.

CAN YOU FIND THESE WORDS ABOUT CITIZENSHIP?

CIRCLE THEM IN THE PUZZLE.

PETITION INTENTION INFORM FREEDOM VERIFY

```
T  P  E  T  I  T  I  O  N  E
U  H  O  Y  N  U  Q  F  P  U
V  O  WK  T  T  I  P  A  G
E  E  F  R  E  E  D  O  M  N
R  T  T  A  N  MP  E  L  O
I  B  C  Y  T  V  J  D  H  T
F  M  R  B  I  WM  T  V  Q
Y  Y  U  K  O  G  V  Z  P  H
V  X  L  I  N  F  O  R  M  E
E  Z  G  U  L  D  X  M  L  Y
```


H. Put five of today's words or word groups from Parts B and C into statements. Underline the vocabulary word or words that you are using.

I. Place any form of five of today's vocabulary words or word groups into questions you would ask someone who works with naturalization papers.

J. Write a paragraph to tell what you read about citizenship records.

K. Prepare a letter to a friend, telling him or her why you think it would be interesting to search for your immigrant ancestor's naturalization records.

L. Today you are going to become a citizen. What are your feelings? Write your thoughts.

M. Have fun with this crossword puzzle.

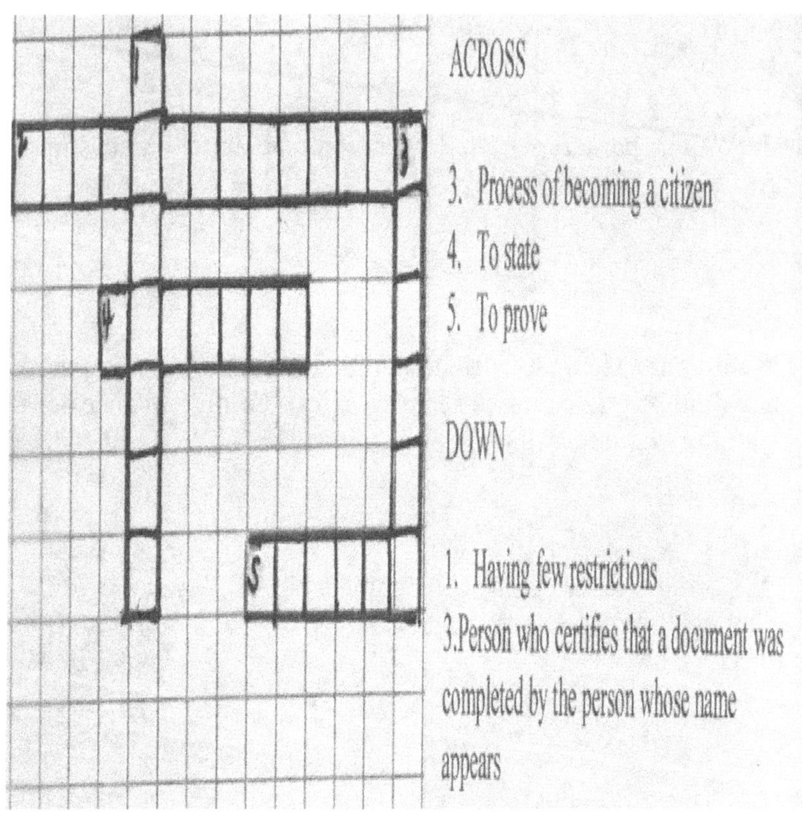

7. *How can a census help you find where the family lived?*

A. Look at the sample Federal census form.

Write a sentence to explain the census item that seems most interesting to you.

B. Read these words or word groups that are in the reading
selection:

     annual
     enumeration
     migrate
     mother tongue
     nativity
     tongue
     township
     trade

C. Now read the paragraphs.

Counting people began a long time ago. Officials in ancient Rome took censuses to see how many people ***migrated*** into the area and how much property they had. That was how the leaders set taxes. The first North American census was in Mexico. In 1749 Benjamin Franklin took a census of the homes in Philadelphia. The British wanted these ***enumerations*** or numbers so they could plan for the future of the colonies. Through the years censuses have been taken in other places such as the Austro-Hungarian Empire, Lithuania, Hungary, Turkey, and Poland.

The early leaders in U.S. history knew that taking a regular census would be a great help with planning for the country's future. Article One, Section Two of The United States Constitution, says that the census must be taken every 10 years. It was not going to be an annual activity. The first official United States census was in 1790. It showed how many people lived in every part of the new country. This information was needed to see how many seats would be in the House of Representatives. They wanted fair, equal representation. Every 10 years it is determined which places have more people living in them. Those with population increases are given more representatives. However, if the population goes down, they may lose representatives. Boundary lines are drawn, based on the census results. The census helps decide how much money should go into schools, roads, helping poor people and creating other projects in all states, townships, and cities. Until 1960 most U.S. censuses were taken door-to-door. Now people get census forms in the mail.

The United States censuses from 1850 to 1930 asked for much information. It included the person's name, sex, color, age, address, **nativity** or birthplace, **trade** or occupation and whether he or she could read and write. Other questions were added or removed in different censuses. Often the enumerator, or census interviewer, asked for the person's **mother tongue.**

Federal censuses records can be found in the National Archives in Washington D.C., in regional archives and on the Internet. You will feel excited when you find ancestors in the censuses. There will be so much information for you.

D. Write any two vocabulary words or groups from the vocabulary list or reading passage. Next to each one write what you think the meaning is.

E. List three vocabulary words or word groups that you do not know. Look in the glossary for the definitions. Write the meanings on the lines next to each word on your list.

F. Find the answers to these questions.

1. The <u>main idea</u> of this reading selection is that
    a. they take a census in Rome.
    b. censuses taken in distinct parts of the world in different time periods could give you facts about your ancestors.
    c. Benjamin Franklin took a census in Philadelphia.
    d. many countries around the world have censuses.

2. Enumerations are
    a. listings of annual activities.
    b. numbers.
    c. trade records.
    d. language lists.

3. According to the passage
    a. there were no censuses before 1749.
    b. the first United States census began late in the 19th century.
    c. the enumeration is also called the census interviewer.
    d. none of the above are true.

4. The author discusses the following facts about the census,
<u>except</u> this:
  a. Census records are difficult to find.
  b. The census helps to directly decide on the future
  political parties of a country.
  c. The first North American census was in Mexico.
  d. In 1790 the United States had its first official
  census.

5. You can see from the paragraphs that
  a. census taking started in modern times.
  b. results of censuses never play a role in government.
  c. censuses helped determine the types of lives your
  ancestors lived.
  d. it is obvious that census-taking is unnecessary.

G. Have fun with this genealogy word search.

CAN YOU FIND THESE WORDS ABOUT THE CENSUS?
CIRCLE THEM IN THE PUZZLE.

ANNUAL MIGRATE TONGUE TOWNSHIP TRADE

```
T R A D E C Q P J E
U H O Y S U Q F P U
T O W N S H I P A G
O E W D N W S D Y N
N T T A N N U A L O
G B C A V V A D H T
U M R B R W M T V Q
E Y U K B G V Z P H
V X L M K B I U K E
E Z G M I G R A T E
```

H. Put any form of five of today's vocabulary words or word groups into statements. Put a line under the vocabulary word or words that you are using.

I. Place five of today's words or word groups from Sections A or B into questions you would ask a person who has just given a speech about census history.

J. Write a paragraph to tell what you read about old census records.

K. Create a letter to a friend, inviting him or her to go with you to do research in census records.

L. Write a true <u>or</u> make-believe story for one of these titles:

"I Found Them in the Census"
"Alone in the 1900 Census"
"They Lived There"
"Searching the Census"
"Answers in the Census"

8. *Will your relatives from the past be listed in a city directory?*

A. Look at the page of a Norwich, Connecticut City Directory from 1904. Write a sentence that tells what information is on the page.

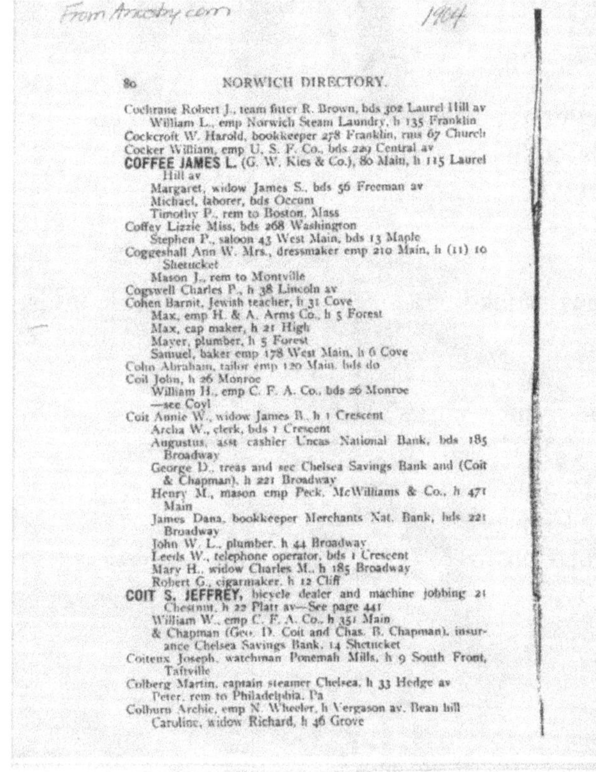

80   NORWICH DIRECTORY.

Cochrane Robert J., team fitter R. Brown, bds 302 Laurel Hill av
    William L., emp Norwich Steam Laundry, h 135 Franklin
Cockcroft W. Harold, bookkeeper 278 Franklin, rms 67 Church
Cocker William, emp U. S. F. Co., bds 229 Central av
COFFEE JAMES L. (G. W. Kies & Co.), 80 Main, h 115 Laurel
    Hill av
    Margaret, widow James S., bds 56 Freeman av
    Michael, laborer, bds Occum
    Timothy P., rem to Boston, Mass
Coffey Lizzie Miss, bds 268 Washington
    Stephen P., saloon 43 West Main, bds 13 Maple
Coggeshall Ann W. Mrs., dressmaker emp 210 Main, h (11) 10
    Shetucket
    Mason J., rem to Montville
Cogswell Charles P., h 38 Lincoln av
Cohen Barnit, Jewish teacher, h 31 Cove
    Max, emp H. & A. Arms Co., h 5 Forest
    Max, cap maker, h 21 High
    Mayer, plumber, h 5 Forest
    Samuel, baker emp 178 West Main, h 6 Cove
Cohn Abraham, tailor emp 120 Main, bds do
Coil John, h 26 Monroe
    William H., emp C. F. A. Co., bds 26 Monroe
    —see Coyl
Coit Annie W., widow James R., h 1 Crescent
    Archa W., clerk, bds 1 Crescent
    Augustus, asst cashier Uncas National Bank, bds 185
        Broadway
    George D., treas and sec Chelsea Savings Bank and (Coit
        & Chapman), h 221 Broadway
    Henry M., mason emp Peck, McWilliams & Co., h 471
        Main
    James Dana, bookkeeper Merchants Nat. Bank, bds 221
        Broadway
    John W. L., plumber, h 44 Broadway
    Leeds W., telephone operator, bds 1 Crescent
    Mary H., widow Charles M., h 185 Broadway
    Robert G., cigarmaker, h 12 Cliff
COIT S. JEFFREY, bicycle dealer and machine jobbing 21
    Chestnut, h 22 Platt av—See page 441
    William W., emp C. F. A. Co., h 351 Main
    & Chapman (Geo. D. Coit and Chas. B. Chapman), insur-
        ance Chelsea Savings Bank, 14 Shetucket
Coiteux Joseph, watchman Ponemah Mills, h 9 South Front,
    Taftville
Colberg Martin, captain steamer Chelsea, h 33 Hedge av
    Peter, rem to Philadelphia, Pa
Colburn Archie, emp N. Wheeler, h Vergason av, Bean hill
    Caroline, widow Richard, h 46 Grove

B. Read these words or word groups that could be used in discussions about city directories.

> accessible
> akin
> corporate records
> correlate
> denote
> format
> household
> occupant
> residence
> resident
> specifics

C. Now read the paragraphs.

Before there were telephone books, there were city directories that were published yearly in the United States in the 1800s and early 1900s. They gave ***specifics*** about people and places in the towns and cities. It was an alphabetical list of adult male ***residents*** and female heads of families. Along with names were occupations and their places of ***residence.*** City directories had business ads that helped people decide what items and services they wanted to use. There were also area maps.

Today you can look through old city directories to find family information.   If you know where an ancestor lived in a specific year, search that city directory. The book can help you find others who were **akin** to that relative because they could have been listed as **occupants** of the same **household**. City directories can help **correlate** with information gathered from censuses.

City directories were also published in areas outside the United States. They were printed in Great Britain's large cities.   Countries including Lithuania, Poland, Russia, and Ukraine had directories in the 20th century.

City directories are easily **accessible.** They are in in books or on microfilm in public libraries, university libraries and the Latter-Day Saints Mormon Family History Library.

The city directory **format** is organized, and important details are **denoted**. Try looking through this source of information. You will agree that it is fun to search through city directories.

D. Write any two vocabulary words or word groups from the word list or reading selection. Next to each one write what you think the meaning is.

E. List three vocabulary words or word groups that are
unfamiliar to you. Look in the glossary for the definitions.
Write the meanings on the lines next to each word on your
list.

F. Find the answers to these questions:

1. The <u>main idea</u> of this reading selection is that
        a. city directories were printed before there were
        telephone books.
        b. there were maps in the city directories.
        c. details about family members from your past can
        be located today in city directories standing on
        different library shelves.
        d. Great Britain published city directories for its large
        cities.
2. Old city directories were like
        a. households.
        b. occupants in big cities.
        c. public libraries.
        d. telephone books.
3. According to the passage
        a. city directories were used before people had
        telephone books.
        b. only males were listed in city directories.
        c. city directories were written in a confusing way.
        d. all the above are true.

4. All of this information is true about city directories,
except this:
   a. City directories were published in many countries
   around the world.
   b. There were no businesses listed in city directories.
   c. You can locate old city directories in different
   libraries.
   d. People's occupations were listed in city directories.

5. The author suggests that
   a. city directories were the ancestors of telephone
   books.
   b. all family members were listed in city directories.
   c. you could find your great-aunt listed as a child in a
   city directory.
   d. it is difficult to search through city directories.

G. Do this matching exercise.

Match each word or word group in Column A with the definition in Column B. Put the letter of the definition in Column B next to the number of the word(s) it matches in Column A.

<table>
<tr><td>A</td><td>B</td></tr>
<tr><td>1. format</td><td>a. business records</td></tr>
<tr><td>2. household</td><td>b. with a common ancestor</td></tr>
<tr><td>3. occupant</td><td>c. people living together in the same apartment</td></tr>
<tr><td>4. specifics</td><td>d. able to get to</td></tr>
<tr><td>5. denote</td><td>e. details</td></tr>
<tr><td>6. correlate</td><td>f. plan of organization</td></tr>
<tr><td>7. accessible</td><td>g. person who lives in a specific place</td></tr>
<tr><td>8. akin</td><td>h. show</td></tr>
<tr><td>9. corporate records</td><td>i. where someone lives</td></tr>
<tr><td>10. residence</td><td>j. go along with</td></tr>
</table>

H. Put any form of five of today's words or word groups from Section A into statements. Put a line under the vocabulary word or words that you are using.

I. Place five of today's words into questions you would ask a librarian about city directories.

J. Write a paragraph that tells what you learned about city directories.

K. Write a letter to a friend about your plans to meet at a library to look through old city directories. Tell what you hope to find when you get there.

L. Write a true <u>or</u> make-believe story for one of these titles:

"I Found a Famous Person from History in the City Directory"

"My Ancestor's Ad in the City Directory"

"I Didn't Know They Lived in the Same House!"

"Clues in the City Directory"

"What I Learned from the City Directory"

M. Complete this crossword puzzle.

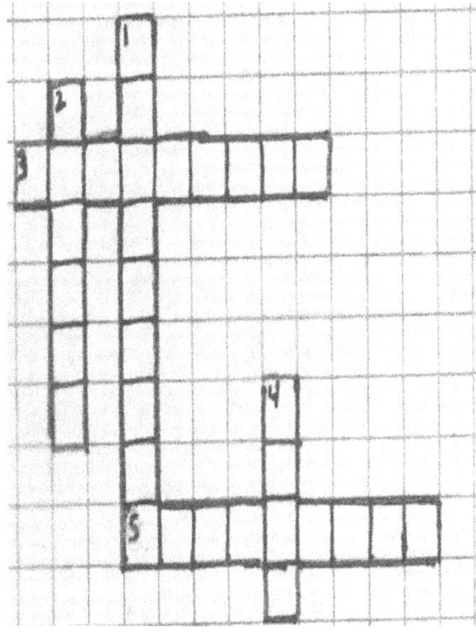

ACROSS

3. People living together in the same apartment of house
5. Details

DOWN

1. People who live in a certain place
2. Way something is organized
4. With a common ancestor

9. *Was anyone in the family a military person?*

A. Prepare a sentence giving your opinion about one branch of the United States Armed Forces.

B. Read these words or word groups that may be used in discussions about the topic of this reading selection.

> citations
> civilian
> date of enlistment
> date of induction
> draft board
> muster rolls
> organizations
> pension
> pensioner
> place of separation
> veterans' benefits

C. Now read the paragraphs.

If you want to learn about family members who were in the United States Armed Forces, there are places to do research. Information is in the National Archives and its branches and in some state archives. Records are also in the National Personnel Records Center in St. Louis, Missouri. The U.S. National Archives and archives in other countries also have military information.

In the U.S. National Archives there are early ***muster rolls*** going back to the year 1801. There is information about ***pensions*** and other ***veterans' benefits*** which were given to the ***pensioners*** between 1775 and 1916.   World War 1 Draft Registration Cards from 1917 and 1918 are available at the National Archives and on some online sites. All men who were native born, naturalized or foreign had to go to the ***draft board*** to fill out those draft registration cards. They had to write their full names. Sometimes their names were signed in their native languages. Each had to tell date and place of birth, as well as race, citizenship, occupation, and a personal description. Similar World War 11 military information is also in the National Archives.

When you learn about a relative's military background you learn if he or she received any ***citations*** or awards. There is a document that was given to everyone who left the military. You should ask your relatives if they can show you their documents. Each stated the person's date of enlistment, the date he or she signed up to join a branch of the military. The document gave the person's date of induction, the date of entry into military service. It shows the ***place of separation*** from the Armed Forces. When you know about a relative's military experiences it can help you understand his or her life after the military days.

You can find records about your family members who may have worked for the military as *civilians*. They are kept at the National Personnel Records Center in St. Louis, Missouri.

Hopefully this information will help you to find information about family members who did some kind of service for the United States Armed Forces.

D. Write any two vocabulary words or word groups. Next to each one tell what you think the meaning is.

E. List three vocabulary words or word groups that are completely unfamiliar to you. Look in the glossary for the definitions. Write the meanings.

F. Find the answers to these questions.

1. The <u>main idea</u> of this reading selection is that
    a. there are ways to learn about family members who were in military services of the United States.
    b. the National Archives has information about pensions and other veterans' benefits.
    c. there were draft registration cards in 1917.
    d. civilians did some military work.

2. One type of benefit for veterans is called a
    a. military service.
    b. place of separation.
    c. pension.
    d. civilian.

3. According to the passage
    a. military records are in the National Archives.
    b. records for civilian workers in the military are impossible to find.
    c. foreign men never had to register for the military.
    d. none of the above are true.

4. The author provides all this information about
     military records, <u>except</u> this:
    a. You can find records for people who were civilians
     working for the military.
    b. One place to find military information is in the
     National Archives.
    c. There were World War 11 draft registration cards
     of 1917 and 1918.
    d. One city with military personnel records is St.
     Louis, Missouri.

5. The author suggests that
    a. military records can never be located in the
     National Archives.
    b. ancestors were not given documents to show when
     they left the military.
    c. not everyone who worked in the military was a
     soldier, sailor, marine or member of the Air Force or
     Coast Guard.
    d. all the draft registration cards were signed in
     English.

G. Try to do this genealogy matching exercise.
*Match each word or word group in Column A with the definition in
Column B. Put the letter of the definition in Column B next to the
number of the word(s) it matches in Column A.*

A	B
1. organizations	a. when one signed up to be in the armed forces
2. date of enlistment	b. person who is not a member of the armed forces
3. veterans' benefits	c. place where a person goes to sign up for the armed forces
4. pension	d. lists of people in a military unit
5. muster rolls	e. when the person started military service
6. civilian	f. where he/she left the military
7. date of induction	g. help with finances, health or education after leaving armed forces
8. citations	h. money that the government regularly sends to retired people from the military
9. draft board	i. awards
10. place of separation	j. clubs

H. Put any form of five of today's vocabulary words or word
groups into statements. Put a line under the word or words that
you are using.

I. Put any form of five of today's words or word groups into questions you would ask someone who has just given a speech about United States military records. Underline the new words you use.

J. Write a paragraph to tell information you can find in military records.

K. You are in the U.S. Army. Write a letter to a relative telling about your life as a soldier.

L. Prepare a diary page about a real or make-believe family member who served in the military and came to visit you.

10. How could you find a newspaper article about a family member from the past?

A. Write a sentence about a section in the newspaper that you think could help you with genealogy research.

B. Read these words or groups of words that are in Section C, the reading selection.

> engagement announcements
> marriage announcement
> obituary
> weekly

C. Now read the paragraphs.

Newspapers can be a wonderful source for getting information about people. They started printing newspapers soon after a group of people settled in a community any place in the world. It is possible to find out names of old newspapers at the Family History Library or on sites online.

People liked to read news about personal events. Births that are listed in local newspapers tell the parents' names, date of birth, the name of the child and sibling information. There are ***engagement announcements*** in all types of newspapers, giving interesting details about the couple. ***Marriage announcements*** appear with names, dates, location of marriage, parents, and honeymoon plans. Military information often appears in print. There are ***obituaries*** in the newspapers. They contain names of individuals who died, with dates, ages, family information and sometimes biographies. Newspapers list funeral ***notices*** telling when and where the event took place. When you look through newspapers you may read articles about school and extracurricular activities performed by students.

While you are studying your family history, it is important to look through old newspapers for information. Remember to save any articles about yourself in a scrapbook. You will enjoy having them and your descendants will love to see your collection.

D. Write any two vocabulary words or word groups. Next to each one tell what you think the meaning is.

E. List three vocabulary words or word groups in the reading selection that you do not know. Look in the glossary for the definitions. Write the meanings on the lines next to each word on your list.

F. Choose the answers to these questions.

1. The <u>main idea</u> of this reading selection is that you can
    a. find birth information in old newspapers.
    b. locate information about ancestors' honeymoon plans in newspapers of the past.
    c. find military information in old newspapers.
    d. search through old newspapers and find different types of news articles about members of your family.
2. Honeymoon plans have often been mentioned in newspaper
    a. marriage announcements.
    b. military articles.
    c. obituaries.
    d. scrapbooks.
3. According to the passage,
    a. birth announcements for family members could have lots of information for you.
    b. the government always wanted military information kept out of newspapers.
    c. you cannot find information about old newspapers in any libraries.
    d. none of the above are true.
4. The author mentions the following newspaper sections that can help with genealogy, <u>except</u>
    a. comics.
    b. engagement announcements.
    c. obituaries.
    d. birth announcements.

5. The writer seems to suggest that
   a. people in the nineteenth century enjoyed watching news on television.
   b. your ancestors probably had an interest in town events.
   c. newspapers are only printed in large European cities.
   d. birth information has never appeared in newspapers.

G. Enjoy this genealogy word search.

Can you find these words about newspapers?
ANNOUNCE MARRIAGE OBITUARY ENGAGED NOTICE
Circle them in the puzzle.

```
A N N O U N C E J E
U H O B S U Q N P U
M O T I S H I G A G
A E W T N W S A Y N
R T T U K N I G L O
R B C A V V A E H T
I M R R R W M D V Q
A Y U Y B G V E P H
G X L M K B I U K E
E Z R U N O T I C E
```

H. Put any form of five of today's vocabulary words or word groups into statements. Put a line under the vocabulary word or words that you are using.

 I. Place five of today's words or word groups into questions you would ask a newspaper writer.

J. Write a paragraph to tell how newspapers can help you with your family history research.

K. Write a letter to a friend, telling him or her why it is interesting to read old newspapers to find information about ancestors.

L. Write a true _or_ make-believe story for one of these titles:

"My Ancestor Was in the News!"

"An Announcement to Remember"

"The Old Newspaper on My Grandparent's Shelf"

"News from Far Away"

"I Remember the Day I Read the Article"

11. *What family information can you locate in Social Security records?*

A. You probably heard people talking about Social Security. Write a sentence to tell what you think it is.

B. Read these words that are in the reading selection.
applicant
employee
maiden
position
unemployed

C. Now read the paragraphs.

In 1935 the Social Security Act was started in the United States. People filled out applications for Social Security cards. Workers who filed Social Security applications could have some money taken out of their pay. That money would be saved for the ***employee***. It would be used to give the person some money each month after he or she reached the age of 65. Today the age requirement has been raised. Because of the Social Security Act, the states can also provide money to disabled and ***unemployed*** people.

The Social Security applications are on record. You can search for relatives through the Social Security Death Index that appears online. It is possible to gather information about a person's date of death and birth. You may find out where the individual first applied for Social Security. You can learn where he or she lived at the time of death, including city, county, state, and zip code.   There is a fee for getting a copy

90

of the application that your ancestors filled out. It could be valuable to you because you can see the person's address at the time of application, place of birth, his or her workplace and job ***position.*** Also included could be the applicant's parents' names.

Sometimes there may be problems locating a relative. A person's surname may have been changed. He or she may have been known by a different first name. If you cannot find a female relative, look under her ***maiden name***.

Social Security information will tell when and where the person died. You can use newspaper sources to find death notices or obituaries. Then you would get more details about the person and the family. You can telephone or write to any listed living relatives. Social Security information can help you find more information about your family's history.

D. Write any two vocabulary words or word groups from Section B or ones that are darkened in the reading selection. Next to each one tell what you think the meaning is.

E. List three vocabulary words or word groups that you do not know. Look in the glossary for the definitions. Write the meanings on the lines next to each word on your list.

F. Decide the answers to these questions:

1. The <u>main idea</u> of this reading selection is that

       a. the Social Security Act was started in the United States in 1935.
       b. you can search for relatives through the Social Security Death Index that appears online.
       c. you can find details about your ancestors who filed applications for Social Security.
       d. workers contribute to Social Security.

2. A retiree is someone who

       a. wants to get a Social Security number.
       b. has an application in the Social Security office.
       c. has a maiden name on her record.
       d. retired from his or her job.

3. According to the passage

> a. the Social Security Act was started in the United States in 1935.
> b. Social Security records are always kept private.
> c. a person's surname stayed the same on all his or her records.
> d. all of the above are true.

4. Each of the following facts about Social Security appear in the reading selection, <u>except</u> this:

> a.   People who contribute money to Social Security can get checks when they retire.
> b. The online Social Security Death Index can help you find information about relatives.
> c. The U.S. Social Security Act was created in the 19th century.
> d. You can pay for a copy of a deceased relative's Social Security application.

5. The author suggests that

> a. workers in the United States were probably glad when the Social Security Act was approved.
> b. the Social Security Death Index does not help you to find additional family information.
> c. Social Security applications are extremely difficult to locate.
> d. if you are lucky enough to find information about a person's Social Security application, you will be happy to see that it can be ordered without a charge.

6. Have fun with this genealogy word search.

CAN YOU FIND THESE WORDS ABOUT SOCIAL SECURITY APPLICATIONS?
CIRCLE THEM IN THE PUZZLE.

APPLICANT POSITION UNEMPLOYED MAIDEN

```
T R A U E C Q P J E
U H O Y S U Q FO U
U N E M P L O YE D
F E M D N WS DY N
A P P L I CA N T O
L B L A V V A D HT
E P O S I T I ONQ
E Y Y K B G V Z P H
V X E M MA I D E N
E Z E U L D XML Y
```

H. Put any form of five of today's words or word groups from Section B into statements. Put a line under the vocabulary word or words that you are using.

I. Place five of the vocabulary words or word groups into questions you would ask someone who works in a Social Security office.

J. Prepare a paragraph that tells how your ancestor's Social Security application can help you know more about his/her life.

K. Write a letter to a friend, talking about something you hope to learn from an ancestor's Social Security application. Explain why that interests you.

L. Write a true <u>or</u> make-believe story for one of these titles:

"Her/His Social Security Application Was a Surprise"

"The Missing Social Security Application"

"His/Her First Job Was Exciting"

"Social Security Information Helped Solve the Mystery"

"Searching for the Answers in a Social Security Application"

12. Will the National Archives have your family's information?

A. You already read about some collections in the National Archives. Write a sentence to explain what information you would like to find in that location.

B. Look at these words that may be used in a discussion of the reading selection.

   abstracts
   archives
   certificate
   deeds
   dependents
   enumerated
   holdings
   inquiry
   issued
   proceedings
   reference staff
   repository
   revenue

C. Now read the paragraphs.

The National *Archives* for the whole United States is in Washington, DC. You can do research there. *Reference staff* members will help if you have an *inquiry.*

In addition to the main building, there are regional branches throughout the United States. Each has *holdings* from the area where it is located. States that have a branch of the National Archives include California, Colorado, Georgia, Illinois, Maryland, Massachusetts, Missouri, New Mexico, New York, Oklahoma, Pennsylvania, Texas, Washington State and Wyoming.

In each *repository* you can find books, as well as records. There are censuses, ship passenger arrival lists and naturalization information. Complete documents and *abstracts* of naturalization court *proceedings* can be found in these archives. Also located in the National Archives are military pension files from 1776-1900 with information about *dependents*. There are *deeds* and other land records, telling where and to whom they were *issued*.

In Canada there is also a National Archives. There are records of Canadian births, adoptions, marriages, divorces, and deaths. They also keep censuses there. The 1901 census records include the date of birth, year of immigration and location of the person's land.

You can copy records at any of the National Archives and be prepared with information to help you add more exciting facts to your family's history.

D. Write any two vocabulary words or word groups. Next to each one tell what you think the meaning is.

E. List three vocabulary words or word groups in Parts A or B that are completely confusing to you. Look in the glossary for the definitions. Write the meanings on the lines next to each word on your list.

F. Find the answers to these questions:
1. The <u>main idea</u> of this reading selection is that you can
    a. search in a National Archives and find a lot of information about your ancestors.
    b. find helpful staff members when you visit the National Archives in Washington, D.C.
    c. go to a regional branch of the National Archives.
    d. search for Canadian information in the National Archives of Canada.

2. A deed is a type of
    a. reference staff.
    b. land record.
    c. proceeding.
    d. dependent.

3. According to the passage
    a. the National Archives for the whole United States is in the state of Washington.
    b. if you go to the National Archives you can get research help from staff members.
    c. only the United States has a National Archives.
    d. none of the above are true.

4. All of the following information can be found in the
United States National Archives, <u>except</u>

     a. copies of school report cards.
     b. censuses.
     c. ship passenger arrival lists.
     d. land records.

5. The passage seems to suggest that

     a. there will be no one to answer your questions in the
National Archives.
     b. you will find Canadian censuses from 1910 in the
Canadian National Archives.
     c. it will not be possible to find passenger arrival lists
in the National Archives.
     d. you should plan to spend a lot of time searching
through much good information in any branch of the
National Archives.

G. Complete this matching exercise.

Match each word or word group in Column A with the definition in Column B. Put the letter of the definition in Column B next to the number of the word(s) it matches in Column A.

<table>
<tr><td>A</td><td>B</td></tr>
<tr><td>1. holdings</td><td>a. people who need others for support</td></tr>
<tr><td>2. deeds</td><td>b. places where records are stored</td></tr>
<tr><td>3. repositories</td><td>c. question</td></tr>
<tr><td>4. revenue</td><td>d. happenings</td></tr>
<tr><td>5. proceedings</td><td>e. people working in the library to help you find information</td></tr>
<tr><td>6. inquiry</td><td>f. documents that transfer ownership of property from seller to buyer</td></tr>
<tr><td>7. enumerated</td><td>g. counted</td></tr>
<tr><td>8. issued</td><td>h. records owned</td></tr>
<tr><td>9. dependents</td><td>i. income</td></tr>
<tr><td>10. reference staff</td><td>j. given to</td></tr>
</table>

H. Put any form of five of today's words or word groups from Section B into statements. Put a line under the vocabulary word or words that you are using.

I. Place any form of five of today's words or word groups into questions you would ask a staff worker in the National Archives.

J. Write a paragraph about holdings in the National Archives.

K. Prepare a letter to a friend, telling him or her about your reasons for doing research in the National Archives.

L. Write a true <u>or</u> make-believe story for one of these titles.

"Searching in the National Archives"

"The Reference Staff Member in the National Archives"

"A Magic Piece of Paper in the National Archives"

"I Found the Information in the National Archives"

"Lost in the Archives"

M. Do this genealogy crossword puzzle.

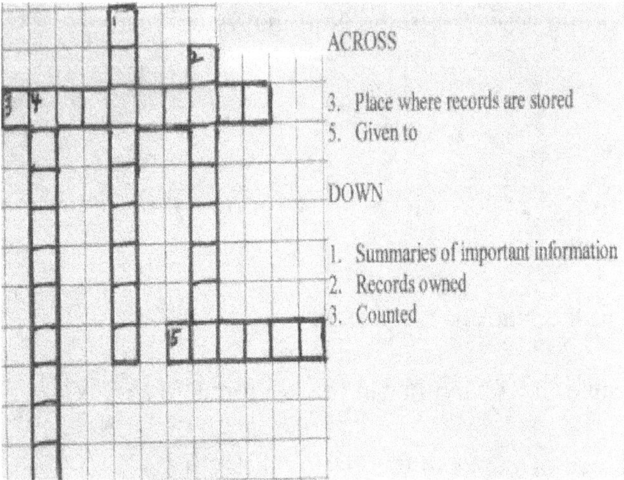

13. Where is the Family History Center and what could it have about your ancestors?

A. In the main *LDS* Family History Library in Salt Lake City, Utah you can find genealogical documents in many languages. Write a sentence telling which language records you would like to search for and tell why.

B. Read these words that will be used in the reading selection.

> fiche
> International Genealogical Index
> locality
> microfiche
> microfilm
> province
> reel

C. Now read the paragraphs.

This *LDS* Family History Library contains many genealogical documents. It is the largest library of its kind in the world and has information about people from all backgrounds.

The Salt Lake City Family History Library has many local branches. One may be near where you live. You can visit it for free and can get help from people there. There may be a translator to help you understand what is written in another language.   Materials not at the local branches can be ordered from the main Family History Library in Salt Lake City, Utah. They will be sent to the branch in your *locality*. Information comes on *reels* of *microfilm*, on *microfiche,* also called *fiche,* and in books.   They have an *International Genealogical Index* database with millions of names.

If you use a personal computer and type in http://www.familysearch.org, you will find the Family History Library Catalog, see what is available and even search for information online.   You could find land, census, court, military and vital records, plus passenger lists.

It is possible to gather much family information from the records supplied by the LDS Family History Library. You can find the address of the building near you by searching the Internet. Happy hunting!

D. Write any two vocabulary words or word groups from Parts B or C. Write what you think the meanings could be.

E. List three vocabulary words or word groups that you cannot explain. Look in the glossary for the definitions. Write what you learn next to each word on your list.

F. Find the answers to these questions:

1. The <u>main idea</u> of this reading selection is that
> a. the LDS Family History Center is in Salt Lake City, Utah.
> b. You can find Family History Center information in many places: in a Family History Library, on microfilm, microfiche, in books and online.
> c. facts about your family can only be discovered in Salt Lake City.
> d. you can find the Family History Library Catalog online.

2. Another word for microfiche is
> a. microfilm.
> b. film.
> c. fiche.
> d. videotape.

3. According to the passage
    a. there are fishing reels at the Family History Center.
    b. geography indexes can help you with genealogy.
    c. the major LDS Family History Library is in Salt Lake City, Utah.
     d. none of the above are true.

4. The author provides all this information about the Family History Center, <u>except </u>this:
    a. It is the largest genealogy library in the world.
    b. Information comes in books, on microfilm and on microfiche.
    c. This library has an International Geographical Index with millions of names.
    d. The LDS Family History Center may have a branch near your town or city.

5. The author suggests that
    a. the LDS Family History Library is the second largest library of its kind in the world.
    b. it would be advisable to do an online search of the Family History Library Catalog before going to a branch of the Family History Library.
    c. if you do not know your ancestor's language, you may not be able to understand the information that is at the Family History Library.
    d. it is difficult to find the addresses for each local Family History Library.

G. Complete this matching exercise.

Match each word or word group in Column A with the definition in Column B. Put the letter of the definition in Column B next to the number of the word(s) it matches in Column A.

A

1. LDS Family History Library

2. microfilm

3. International Genealogical Index

4. locality

5. reel

6. cross-reference

7. province

8. fiche

9. Salt Lake City, Utah

10. Familysearch.org

B

a. website for Family History Library

b. location of main genealogy building

c. division of a country

d. round film holder

e. note at one place to check other places

f. microfiche

g. gigantic database

h. a roll of film with information

i. world's largest genealogy library

j. area

H. Put any form of five of today's words or word groups from Sections B or C into statements. Put a line under the vocabulary word or words that you are using.

I. Place any of five of today's words or word groups into questions you would ask a worker in the Family History Center.

J. What would you like to find in the Family History Center? Write a paragraph.

K. Prepare a letter to a friend, telling him or her why it is a good idea to do research in the Family History Center.

L. Write a true <u>or</u> make-believe story for one of these titles.

"Found in the Family History Center"

"The Microfilm Solved the Mystery!"

"Discovered in a Foreign Language"

"Amazing Find"

"A Library to Remember"

SOME GENEALOGY SITES
ON THE INTERNET

www.rtrfoundation.org
www.familysearch.com
www.ancestry.com
www.genealogy.com
www.myheritage.com
www.findmypast.com
www. National Archives and Records Administration
familyhistory@records.nyc.gov -
(New York City Municipal Archives)
www.loc.gov - (Library of Congress)

Enjoy looking for your family's information on the Internet!

GLOSSARY

abstracts - summaries of important information
access - get into
accessible - able to get to
acquire - get
affidavits - written statements made or taken under oath before a court officer or a notary public
akin - related to, descended from a common ancestor
alias - fake name
alien - a foreign born resident who has not been naturalized and is still a citizen of another country
alluding to - making indirect reference to
ancestor - family member who lived a long time ago
ancestral file – database or collection of family information organized in a computer
ancestry chart - chart that shows family members from the past
anglicized - made to look or sound like English
annual - yearly
appease - to keep peace and quiet
applicant - one who applies for a job
approximate - nearly correct
archives - places where public records or historical documents are preserved
archive - collection of data or files
area - section
articulate - express clearly

brick walls - dead ends in genealogy research

certificate - paper with official information
chronological order – arrangement of events as they happened in time
circa - around (circa 1891= around the year 1891)
citations - honors for excellent work
civilian - person who is not a member of the Armed Forces
common - usual
composite picture - combination of details
conceal - to hide
contemporary - modern
corporate records - business records
correlate - show relationship between two things
cross-reference - a note at one place to check another spot with helpful information

database - organized collection of information on the computer
date of enlistment - date one signed up for a branch of the armed forces
deceased – not living
Declaration of Intention - first paper filed in court stating a person's wish to be a citizen
declare - to state something
deeds - documents that show ownership of property that transfers from seller to buyer
deferred - delayed
deliberate - done on purpose
denote - point out

dependents - people who need others for support

descendancy chart – chart that starts with the ancestor who goes farthest back in time and works downward to the youngest people in the family.

descendant - person's child, grandchild, great-grandchild

destination - where someone or something is going

detain - delay

devise - to plan

directory - type of book

distort - twist out of the original meaning

document - official paper

draft board - place where a person goes to sign up for the armed forces

elusive - hard to find

embark - to go aboard a ship

emerge - to come forth, to become important

emigrants - people leaving a country

emigrate – to leave one's place of residence or country to live someplace else

emigration - act of people leaving a country to settle in another land

employee - worker

engagement announcements - notices about people who plan to get married

enumerated - counted

enumeration - a listing or counting

ethnic groups - people who share the same cultures

evidence - proof

evolution - slow process of change from simple to complex
exact - specific

family group sheet - form that has birth, marriage, death, and burial information about one family unit - father, mother, and children.
family tree - chart that holds the names and basic information about all members of a family- from the oldest to the youngest.
fiche - a sheet of film with very small images of recorded information
final destination - the last place where one plans to go
format - plan of organization
freedom - independence, liberty
Freedom of Information Act - gives people the right to get certain private information

genealogy - study of family history
generation - average span of time between birth of parents and birth of their children

holdings - records owned
household - people living together in the same apartment or house

inadvertent - not intentional
index - list of items in a special order
influx - coming in
informant - one who gives information

inquiry - a question
intention- plan
International Genealogical Index - a database of names taken from original records from all over the world - created and kept by the Latter-Day Saints Family History Library
investigation – a careful study of something, examination
issued - given to

LDS - Latter Day Saints
lineage - group of descendants from a common ancestor
lineage chart - a picture showing relationships between family members
listing - information in a list
locality - area
log - record

maiden - unmarried woman
maiden name - a woman's last name before marriage
mandate - order
manifest - passenger list
mannerisms - ways of speaking or acting
marital status - tells whether a person is married, single, divorced, separated, or widowed
marriage announcement - news about two people who got married
microfiche - a sheet of microfilm with very small images of recorded information

microfilm - a roll of film with a record that is reduced in size
migrate - movement from one area to another
mother tongue - language of one's country of birth
movements - actions
muster rolls - lists of men in a military unit
myth - a false belief

nationality – membership in a particular nation
nativity - place of birth
naturalization - process of becoming a citizen
naturalized - became a citizen
notary (also called notary public) - public officer allowed to guarantee that documents are true
notices - announcements

obituary - notice about a person's death
occupant - one who lives in a specific place
occupation - job
omission - something left out
online - being connected to the Internet
organizations - groups of people with a special purpose

patterns - styles
pedigree chart - a chart including facts about one person's direct ancestors (parents, grandparents, great-grandparents.)
pension - money that the government or a company regularly sends to a retired person as a reward for service
pensioner - one who gets a pension
perished - destroyed
pertained to - was about
petition - a request made to a court
phonetically - by sounds
place of separation – place where a person left military service
pose questions - ask questions
position - job
proceedings - happenings
province - a division of a country

reel - a round holder of film
reference staff - people working in the library to help visitors find information
reliable - dependable
repository - place where records are stored
research form - paper that organizes the information you find - includes date of research, ancestor's name, where the information was found, what was found.
research log - list of dates, sources, and other information that the researcher finds
residence - where one lives

resident - person who lives in a specific place
resources - sources of information
revelations - information that is revealed
revenue - income

section - area
sibling - brother or sister
sites - places
source - where something came from
specifics - details
steamship - a ship that moves by steam power
strategy - way of doing something
supplied - given
surname - family name, last name
system - way to organize

tombstone - stone that marks a grave
tongue - language

township - division of a county
trace - to follow or study details step by step
trade - occupation
truism - truth

unable - not able to do
unemployed - without a job
upheavals - major changes

variants - differences
verify - prove
vernacular language – one's native language, common speech
veterans' benefits - help with finances, health and/or education given to someone after serving in a branch of the armed forces
victims - those who are made to suffer
vital records - birth, marriage, and death documents

weekly - newspaper that comes out once a week
White Pages - telephone listings of residents in the area
WWW - World Wide Web

Yellow Pages - business telephone and address listings

ANSWER KEY

LESSON 1 - Family History
F. 1.b   2.c   3.a   4.c   5.a
G. 1.k   2.i   3.h   4.g   5.f   6.e   7.d   8.c   9.b
10.a   11.j

LESSON 2 - Interviews
F. 1.d   2.d   3.d   4.a   5.c
G. 1.e   2.j   3.a   4. i   5.d   6.h   7.f   8.g   9.c
10.b   11.k

LESSON 4 – Birth-Marriage-Death
F. 1.b   2.b   3.d   4.b   5.a
G. 1.b   2 i   3.a   4.e   5.g   6.d   7.f   8.j   9.c   10.h

LESSON 5 - Immigration
F. 1.b   2.d   3.d   4.c   5.b
G. 1.g   2.i   3.f   4.e   5.d   6.h   7.b   8.j   9.a
10.c

LESSON 6 - American Citizen
F. 1.d 2.a   3.d   4.c   5.b

LESSON 7 - Census
F. 1.b   2.b   3.d   4.a   5.c

LESSON 8 – City Directory
F. 1.c   2.d   3.a   4.b   5.a
G. 1.f   2.c   3.g   4.e   5.h   6.j   7.d   8.b   9.a   10.i

LESSON 9 - Military
F. 1.a   2.c   3.a   4.c   5.c
G. 1.j   2.a   3.g   4.h   5.d   6.b   7.e   8.i   9.c   10.f

LESSON 10 - Newspaper
F. 1.d   2.a   3.a   4.a   5.b

LESSON 11 – Social Security
F. 1.c   2.d   3.a   4.c   5.a

LESSON 12 – National Archives
F. 1. a   2.b   3.b   4.a   5.d
G. 1.h   2.f   3.b   4.i   5.d   6.c   7.g   8.j   9.a
10.e

LESSON 13 – Family History Center
F. 1.b   2.c   3.c   4.c   5.b
G. 1.i   2.h   3.g   4.j   5.d   6.e   7.c   8.f 9.b   10.a